WAKE UP
AND
LIVE
in Love

Arliss Beabout

BALBOA.PRESS
A DIVISION OF HAY HOUSE

Balboa Press books may be ordered through booksellers or by contacting:

Balboa Press
A Division of Hay House
1663 Liberty Drive
Bloomington, IN 47403
www.balboapress.com
1 (877) 407-4847

Because of the dynamic nature of the Internet, any web addresses or links contained in this book may have changed since publication and may no longer be valid. The views expressed in this work are solely those of the author and do not necessarily reflect the views of the publisher, and the publisher hereby disclaims any responsibility for them.

The author of this book does not dispense medical advice or prescribe the use of any technique as a form of treatment for physical, emotional, or medical problems without the advice of a physician, either directly or indirectly. The intent of the author is only to offer information of a general nature to help you in your quest for emotional and spiritual well-being. In the event you use any of the information in this book for yourself, which is your constitutional right, the author and the publisher assume no responsibility for your actions.

Any people depicted in stock imagery provided by Getty Images are models, and such images are being used for illustrative purposes only. Certain stock imagery © Getty Images.

Print information available on the last page.

Scripture taken from the Amplified Bible, Copyright © 1954, 1958, 1962, 1964, 1965, 1987 by The Lockman Foundation. Used with permission.

ISBN: 978-1-9822-3659-5 (sc)
ISBN: 978-1-9822-3661-8 (hc)
ISBN: 978-1-9822-3660-1 (e)

Library of Congress Control Number: 2019916087

Balboa Press rev. date: 10/26/2019

Dedication

For all those that cry in the night, waiting for the sweet light of dawn with the new hope of a better day this is for you.

Know that you are not alone and that we all face the same discovery of self to find fulfillment.

With great respect and honor to my husband who never doubted what I had to say and supporting all that would be entailed to bring this work to pass.

To my Mother, Jeanette who taught me courage and most of all Love. My greatest mentor and friend whom I miss dearly but, is never too far away.

I pray that blessing and knowledge come to you and inspire and give you fortitude to pursue that which is rightfully yours.

To our beloved Heavenly Father that always finds a way, better than we ever could have expected or imagined.

The fulfiller of all our dreams.

Contents

Prologue

An ordinary girl doing an extraordinary thing. Where can I begin to explain the process of reveal-meant. I spent many years believing I had faith and that alone would sustain me day to day.

I was having miracles happen but, not really enjoying the meaning of the full manifesting. Some days had become so robotic. I was caught up in the world and what it wanted me to do that I forgot to consider what I should be doing. After the death of my mother in 2008, the desire to be more aware and give something back became overwhelming. So I set out to get the answers I needed.

I was led to the study of Kabbalah to find those answers; mind you I was brought up protestant, Baptist, Christian. Again I had faith but I had no idea what to do with it.

With Kabbalah I found the tools and the consciousness I was lacking. I can say it was as if a dam had broken loose. I had been asleep.

So journey with me as I share with you how I woke up from a deep sleep into a life full of joy, miracles & most of all Love.

And so it begins

Finding out what you are and all that comes with you to this earth is the most fascinating adventure of all.

We all have angels, but do we know who they are, why they are here to help. I have learned of mine and upon waking up I now connect with them as much as possible in all of life's decisions.

I have always listened to my inner spirit, gut feeling. But, have not heeded its call many times. In the times that I have; success is always the outcome. I started to wonder who are these angels whose soul job is to make sure I finish a path of predestination I started. First you have to accept you did set up the path you have lead, but then the opportunity to make it something wonderful and different was never part of the equation. Now I see that it is and can be anything you want it to be. So where to start is the question everyone has.

We all have been in places and situations that we desperately want to rid ourselves of, but do your account for your choice to be there. First step is accepting total responsibility for self.

I do not blame anyone for my situations; this frees up your spirit from obsessing and prompting the same situation again and again. This is painful and difficult but, can be done day by day minute by minute. In this realm of mind you free up your ego and allow your soul to direct your choices.

Bondage comes in many forms starting with the ones you are taught from birth on how to behave, how much money to make, what type of person you should marry, the car you should drive and the list goes on and on. . ... Just filter that thought alone and see where it leads you.

I felt controlled by this, not truly doing or thinking about what I wanted. This opened me up to options and choices I believed I never had, the lie of the Ego.

Once I began to expose my ego from an objective point of view, not one of self-loathing, I saw all the tentacles and how they had attached themselves to me. Now the work is in cutting off those tentacles that hide and obscure who my true self is. Will this be easy, no and I will not tell you it is. It is a process that you must become committed to, there is no two second fix and you will have to start visualizing yourself as something else not what you used to think defines who you are.

You will expose a self that you never knew existed and you will like them and then you will fall in Love with them. . ...

Why, because you were always perfect, you just did what you thought and were taught was the self to be.

Say hello to the new you. . .

Patience my Love

The creator has control on this one hands down. God cannot be rushed for everything he does is perfect. . . ..

In this hurry world be live in. Wanting everything right now, say patience to someone and they want to laugh or run you over. We have to stop and live in the present moment.

Do you really know if this is you last moment or not. I have learned now to live each day without regrets. Tell your family today you Love them, give your kids an extra hug before they leave for school, make that phone call to the friend you haven't seen in years. What that extra minute of time you take today may guarantee you a better tomorrow.

We live in a society where most things are disposable, people are not and learning that when they are gone is far more painful.

Know that everything you do is related to everyone you know and come in contact with daily. There is no randomness out of perfected order. We just have to wake up to see the order of it. Once you allow yourself to see this, your vision will take on a completely different landscape.

As they say in Kabbalah "you can change your movie" you are the director!

This was extremely profound to me because I always saw

myself as powerless not powerful. I had to completely shift my thinking from maybe to defiantly. Learn to dream again, get back your childlike nature. Why do you think children amaze us so much? Because they are not polluted with the lies of this world yet. They are perfect and show the self of our creator through them.

Your Magnet

A magnet (from Greek "Magnesium stone") is a material or object that produces a magnetic field. This magnetic field is invisible but is responsible for the most notable property of a magnet: a force that pulls on other ferromagnetic materials, and attracts or repels other magnets. [1]

So we all have two parts to our magnet, the love side and the ego side. When these two forces are not joined together there is space. This space creates a place for other parts of the magnet to either attract or repel. Simply put which side are you giving your force to.

One of the parts of our journey is to close the space and be in perfect union so that your true self is in control of your life and not the ego. We are always seeking balance.

We spend so much time putting up walls so people will see us the way we think they should instead of being our true self and not caring if people like it or not.

Being who your true self is can only come from a place of love because you were created out of love, but how do we find our way back to our core? This is the greatest work.

Changing the myths and concepts that we are raised to believe takes great concentration and effort to undo. So we start by taking one step at a time removing the layers of doubt and preconceived notions that we have all grown up with. Opening our hearts to a change that will bring a result greater than us.

Example: if you grew up being told you will never be good enough or that you will always be too thin or to fat, how long have you accepted this to be true? Think about how you really feel. You waste no effort changing any of those because you have just accepted that is the way it is......But I am here to tell you that they are all lies. Are you willing to make a change and prove the lies to be wrong? You can be anything you want to be!

Where is your heart regarding these lies, a spark of faith can change I Can't too I can do anything or I can lose weight or better yet I look great! When this resonates inside then you can begin the transformation of the heart regarding the old lies.

This is where the work begins because you have to start talking to yourself differently. You cannot keep playing the same recording in your head and expect the result to change.

This recording is playing all day long over many insidious little lies that we continue to hang on to. What happens next the fear creeps in and that recording starts telling you, that you will never change, why make yourself uncomfortable, don't upset the apple cart blah blah blah......

See where I am going with this. Think about how many decisions you make all day long. From the moment we wake in the morning we start with what to eat, when to leave for work, what's for lunch, what am I going to do this weekend, what's for dinner tonight etc.?

Nowhere in that space of time did you say anything to yourself appreciating one that you have another day, or telling yourself you are loved as you are and that you will face the day in love, and thank the creator for today.

No one should face any day without this affirmation. This creates the place for your force and to close the space in your magnet, to keep the external forces out. Then you will feel your balance. Stop giving away your energy to useless nonsense that gives you no purpose.

Why Intent

Intention is a powerful word, and a powerful action. This will determine much of what you experience in this life the hard way or the way of Love and wonder and knowledge. Everything we do has an intention. Stop for a moment and think about this. What was your desired intent with calling your friend today? To really say Hi, how are you? Or if I call today I know they will want to get together this weekend, they are great they always pick up the tab on our outings. I call this "achieves to receive method". The egos screaming out me, me, me. ...We spend too much time focusing on ourselves and not enough time on others. When we give of ourselves all of our needs are met. You would have to try this to know what I am talking about. This not only creates balance, it is full filling in more ways than I can mention.

There are so many ways we can give of ourselves the list is endless. Every action counts no matter how small or how grand. This has to be conditioned into our life. when you start paying attention to these areas you will be amazed how it all is inter-connected and the magnificent impact it can have on your life and everyone else's.

This is not something you have to train for, you have to retrain you thinking, this will become effortless you just have to practice.

Awaken

$\mathcal{J}$ust be open to the endless possibilities available and accessible for you. There is so much in this world for us to love and enjoy, we just have to start doing it together and stop separating ourselves from others. We are all looking for our purpose. Question is, are you ready to wake up? Tired of being on auto pilot with no plan, feeling hopeless, or that nobody loves you.

One of the hardest things you will ever do is to really love yourself for who you are and be more than ok with that.

Once you really come to a place where you know this without any doubt, pay attention how differently everybody else pays attention to you. The love you wanted or respect from others flows to you like a magnet. You have closed that space in your magnet. You are more focused on others instead of yourself and you love yourself unconditionally.

Guess what happens next, people see this in you and want what you have, now what, share, share, share! What price can any of us put on that kind of true self freedom?

Remember those layers I told you about, they start to peel away like a beautiful rose unfolding. You will like who you see when you get to the core. Because its real and it is your true beauty, which no one can duplicate you are the only copy.

On this you can begin to see the purpose of your being and all that you have to offer this world. Start with your family and work is the greatest practice ground for all of this because of the diversities in personalities that are around us.

If I can do it I know you can! Can I share a little story with you? About four years ago I really felt a heaviness on my heart to find my purpose and what can I contribute to this world. I am not a famous Doctor I am not an actor or TV personality etc. What difference could little ole' me make? Well the universe is great because there is a lot to be said about "ask and it shall be given, seek and you shall find".

Many teachers and books just seemed to find their way to me and help me on my awakening; I changed my thinking and began to really concentrate on the areas in my life that I wanted to change. Nothing like going for the hard stuff right, I choose to tackle my weight. All my life I have carried around those extra 50-65 pounds. Why? Believing the lie, you'll never lose weight and if you do you will gain it right back and you will never look like that and on and on. I kept that lie alive for 30 years. What a waste of time.

But, because I had awakened to my true self, it told me I will succeed and nothing is impossible only you can stop you from having what you truly desire. So Off I went on my diet, and I have to tell you it was a breeze, why because my thinking changed my true self was in charge not my ego. I learned to enjoy the diet and how to eat in a healthy manner. Really searched to find my triggers for gaining. Needless to say it is carbs. Love Rice and sauces. So now that is my desert and I can only have them on occasion and I plan for them. I found that six small meals a day for me is great and I think I am cheating because I am always eating. But I love what I am eating and best of all I am not a slave to food anymore.

Again what price can you put on this kind of freedom? This is just one example. But we have many areas in our life that can be handled in the same manner. Question is do you really want to be free or just keep having the same conversation about it. . . .. Over and over again?

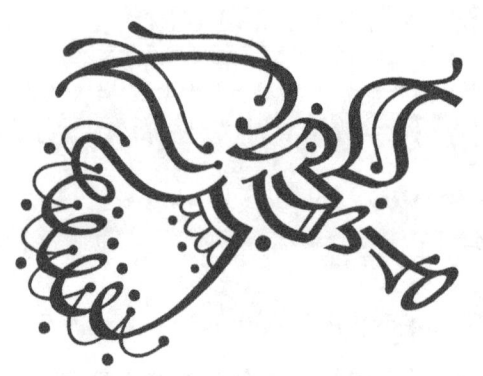

Mountains

Why the mountains. Well because this is how to grow up to be spiritual giants. We can't stay babies forever. We are all here to help each other. One thing that rings true is you cannot help anybody else until you help yourself.

Perfect example of this is people that have been through traumatic events in their lives and then go on to be great consoulers for others from their tragedy. This is what binds all of us together. So we can inspire and heal each other.

This is just one big class room and we are all still in the school of life as long as there is breath in us. Death is graduation and I want to graduate on the Dean's list how about you?

Manifestation

We are all artist, how is your movie looking to you? How do you see the rest of your movie playing out? What are you deepest desires? Can you hear the internal voice of your soul calling out to you?

These are the questions we all face at some point in our life, can we find the courage to address them or continue to keep them hidden as if they do not exist.

First let us address what we are. Do you believe you are a being of spirit in a physical body or a physical body that is or will become spirit? The answer is being of spirit in a physical body. You are spirit first and that is our origin of birth. Your journey here is to reconcile the body to the spirit to accomplish the soul's desire for evolvement. Did I lose you with that one?

Deep I know. But, with learning through embracing this concept you will never be alone again or feel that you have no value or purpose in this life. When we are born we are as close to the spirit as possible then as we grow we lose some of the child like spirit because we become entrenched in the world and how it operates and we are taught how we are to operate in it as well. Then the conflict begins inside of us, because somehow we have become separated from the place that internally we know is home (our spirit). Our true life or journey then begins as we try to reclaim what was lost. How do we know this? Do you have those feelings of hunger but for what? Are you feeling like a clock is ticking but for what? Does any sense of urgency press you? These are the questions that many of us face as we try to live in this world of want and material desires that continue to leave us unfulfilled.

We need to come back to the true source of our being and heal the pieces that have been lost through our experiences that only the creator with his grace can and will make whole.

We have everything we need to overcome the world inside of us if we choose to tap into it. There really is no great mystery to this only different translations. But one thing I believe we can all agree on is Love is always the greatest source of healing and truth.

Even without the spiritual side of it, we all want to be loved and cared for. Why is this so, this is the cord that attaches us to the creator who is love in all of its forms.

But the question still remains how we can bring this into our lives to not only help ourselves but heal the world in return?

So what is love?

So let's start from the beginning with something all or most of us have heard before. Corinthians 13:4 thru 7.

4) Love endures long as is patient and kind; love never is envious nor boils over with jealousy, is not boastful or vainglorious, does not display itself haughtily.

Well how did you do? Do these things represent your life and your behavior? Are you patient and kind? Do you now look at others with jealousy? Are you full of pride?

This is an opportunity for you to consider how you want to represent yourself in the world, are these things at the top of your list on a daily basis. Are you kind to your children, your fellow employees or your spouse. We all have these things to deal with but the good news is we are more than capable to overcoming these basic life changing steps that can open the universe up to you, to bring blessing and prosperity into everything that you do because these are the how to do it principals. Simply put, I change myself and everything around me changes too. Let's read on.

5) It is not conceited (arrogant and inflated with pride): it is not rude (unmannerly) and does not act unbecomingly. Love (God's love in us) does not insist on its own rights or

its own way. For it is not self-seeking; it is not touchy or fretful or resentful; it takes no account of the evil done to it (it pays no attention to a suffered wrong).

Ok how did you do with that one? Can you see the correlation of our behaviors and attitudes could have something to do with why we have difficult times in our life or are at odds with someone on a continual basis? Do these types of situations make you comfortable or are they a constant source of aggravation for you? Well my friend you do not have to live this way anymore. But, it will take a conscious decision on your part to change it. I myself had a very hard time with this. What do you mean I have to change they are the one being rude, giving me attitude. Yes but, the answer here is; should that offend me, why should I lower my behavior to their level. I walk in love and I will not be rude and I will not take offense when people make off handed comments or try to hurt my feelings. Why because these moments in time do not in any way define your true greatness. It is only a test. Can you pass?

A lot of retraining your thinking will bring you to the place where you can react in this manner and know who and what you truly are. Let's go on to the next verse.

6) It does not rejoice at injustice and unrighteousness, but rejoices when right and truth prevail.

7) Love bears up under anything and everything that comes is ever ready to believe the best of every person, its hopes are fadeless under all circumstances, and it endures everything (without weakening).

I love these last two verses especially because there is your answer to everything. Love can handle anything this world can dish out and you'll overcome and will not be weak because of it.

Consider this your pearl of wisdom; try to embrace this all too familiar words with a fresh and renewed mind. This will change everything in your life, no matter where you are or what you are doing. This is for everyone. No one person is singled out and there is no special club membership to join.

This just works!

So let's travel back to the beginning. Where are you on your spiritual quest? I started out Christian but the way religion is taught it is boring and uneventful. But, inside I knew there was something greater than me and thinking back have experienced nothing short of miracles in my life. I would not consider myself and overly religious person, if anything I would say I rebel. I wanted something that spoke to my soul and gave me tools with knowledge of how I should operate in this world until my end. More than that I wanted to give back all the wonderful blessings in my life and the freedom I now found. This was not taught to me in any church, it came from my soul.

For me it was Kabbalah that answered my many unanswered questions I had and I could easily blend it with the Christian back ground. This has enhanced my faith tremendously.

Basically I took the religiosity out of it back to the raw core of its original creation and intent. I believe now that I have the creators true purpose in my heart and soul not man's version of it.

Who is your GOD?

What does your version of God look like is it Hindu, Buddha, Muslim, Baptist, Catholic, Jewish. What is the one identifying marker of all these. They were created out of Love.

Unfortunately over time many restrictions have been applied to all of these, again are they leaving you faithless? I knew I believed but I did not know how to believe. When was I going to have this great relationship they all talk about, this personal one on one with God? Well, I had to go look for myself and stop asking someone else to do it for me. Yes, that's what I said; and yes it hurt me to when I came to the realization. I am responsible for me. No one else was going to be able to this for me I had to go seek for myself.

Again the universe is so on target, it will bring to you what you need when you ask, you just have to act upon it. So should we get into the coincidence discussion. Here me now, there is no such thing as Luck or coincidence, everything is perfectly orchestrated for your arrival on stage sort to speak. The question you should be asking is do I acknowledge the sign that is being given?

If you take the time to think back at all the monumental

events in your life how did they arrive for you and what did you take away from it. Some things are really beyond explanation. That is another fact I have come to live with, I do not need to know everything about everything. I just have to do what I am lead to do and that all things will work out to my best interest because that is my intention.

The Power of Intention

So let's talk simply about this word intent. Webster's (2) dictionary describes this word as: Intention; aim; a plan; firmly fixed or directed upon. Wow I love the way that sounds, there is no wavering on intent. This should be our daily goal. Take that same intent and re-direct it to being more loving with my spouse or children. Or being more patient with my boss at work who makes me nuts. Remember they cannot make you nuts, you allow them to make you nuts. Don't forget about your free will. These sound so simple yet daily we are faced with these little nuances that have us make decisions on our behavior. The guy that cuts you off in traffic, are you going to cuss him out or just let it roll of your back. Your only goal in a car should be God get me to where I am going safely, that's it.

As we go through the day we have to make constant little decisions on our reactive behaviors. Why do I call it that because if you think about it, remember the ones that are pleasant and remember the ones that were not so pleasant? What was the outcome? How long did your bad response upset you for the rest of your day into the night? Why?

If you remember anything that I have said remember this:

No one can own you, and <u>no one can take your soul from you.</u>

Start making decisions that enhance your life and those that are around you.

Why do I have to do everything?

And the answer is because you have freedom of choice. As you start on your journey of self-discovery you will find that many things are already in you. You are born perfect, but somehow we are diluted and dis-illussioned that we are inferior and will never amount to much. Some of us have had this in bigger doses than others. I am pretty safe to say that most of us have had this mentality feed to us by employers, family and friends. Well, I am here to tell you again you have a choice to stay this way or change it. Because God is so awesome and knew that someday you would be asking these questions. The part that is so exciting, you already have everything you need, we now just have to learn to activate and facilitate so we can illuminate our greatness!

Opening yourself up to a new way

So now you know you have it, so let's go find it. Start allowing yourself to investigate and explore different ways of spiritual growth. You will know when you have found the path that works for you, your soul and your heart will sing.

For me it was Kabbalah, because I tend to be so logical and want everything explained. I want to know who, what, where and when. But, with that being said I have also learned that I do not have to know everything. This has lead me to a greater appreciation for the creator and that everything really is ok in the universe. "I do not need to control everything" nor can I for that matter; learned that the hard way.

We become so robotic that we withdraw ourselves from the very things that could give us the most pleasure, beauty and love that this wonderful world has to offer. Your mind has controlled you for so long that the thought of not listening to it is frightening. We "think" we know it all. Unfortunately this is not so, and the universe will use whatever means it has to till it gets your full attention. That is why you need to follow through on your quest and not wait till it is a dire straits situation.

I have found the journey to be very enlightening and comforting all at the same time. Because I have a destination now, what I do is no longer about me anymore it is about all of us.

We have all come from a place where "Love Rules" and that is the deepest desire inherent in all of us. We all crave it regardless of the form it comes in.

Well, "What about Me"

Have you worn yourself out yet? I woke up one day and was sick and tired of wondering what about me. In learning to reconnect to people and appreciating the good that is already present in my life, this is not my question anymore. I now ask what I can do for you. I know what Jesus meant when he said "Love thy neighbor as thyself". For when I put others first, all And I mean all of my needs are met! I know that sounds way too simple but, that is it. To take it one step further there are only two things that you need to do and that is "Love the Creator God with all you heart and soul & "Love thy neighbor as thyself" and all these things shall be added unto you! Yes that means everything, not partial not just a little bit. . .all of it!

The Secrets of your Heart

Now this is where your spiritual work comes in. You must be true inside and your intentions pure. Double mindedness does not work. You will never achieve spiritual greatness if you are indecisive and constantly flipping your decisions. Even if you make a mistake, you can then go back and do it differently. We cannot become fearful of Loving to the point we do the opposite and continue to keep ourselves locked up. Don't you miss that childlike quality of wanting to know and try everything? You can adapt this kind of attitude towards your own self-discovery. A decision will come out of everything you do, you like it or you don't. Then just say "Next"… Just keeping moving forward, don't look back and do not lay a guilt trip on yourself as well. Yes those lies will continue to pop up from time to time. But, you must learn to say NO!

You Are Not Alone

So let's talk about that special team that has been assigned to you. Do you know you have an entire team of angels just waiting to hear from you and you alone? Your Guardian angel who has been with you since birth is with you till the day you leave this earth. As well as possible past family members from previous lives or this one. Also the Arch Angels and ascended masters are all here for you to request assistance from.

With deep love please believe when I say you are never alone, no matter what is happening in your life right now. No matter what anyone says to you. All you have to do is ask and your team is on the scene now. . . . They will give you strength when you feel you have none left. They will protect you in times of great danger. They listen when no one else will listen. Most of all They Love you like no one can love you because, God made them just for you. . . . . You may find that hard to swallow but, let that soak in and we will touch on that again later.

So Can You See Yourself
In A Different Light

How do you look to yourself now, any possibility that you could be different? Are you willing to change one small thing at time to be that different person you have dreamed of, but, are too afraid to even attempt to become? Because, when you start walking on this spiritual path of growth, you will start dreaming of all kinds of things to become, and some will have you so excited that you will not be able to contain your new exciting self. Yes it is possible and you will feel it rise up inside of you in a place that you thought never existed for you. You can step out of that darkness to a place of light and magic. The only thing stopping you is fear. Trust me when I say this we all have it just in varied degrees. Some of us have just gotten better at shooing it away quicker. This will take time but, you can master that also.

One day you will look back and not even recognize the person you were. These little steps of faith made daily for the rest of our lives moves into the perfection for which we came here to begin with. Your life is not for nothing. You are such an important part of this earth's time and evolution you could not even begin to understand right now. You will get it, as I have...

This Is What The Creator Was After

We are here to help each other and ourselves. Our souls that are so much smarter than us planned this whole agenda/journey that we are currently on. You participated first hand in the options and choices that were and are to come into your life for your soul's advancement. Nothing is coincidental and hap hazard. You will learn as I have that this beautiful orchestration of life is just that a very well thought out and **perfected illustration of Love.**

Why Am I Having Such a Hard Time Believing?

Well to answer that question, let's talk about the flesh. Jesus said "the spirit is willing the flesh is weak". Bottom line that is your ego. That part of you that knows it all, the arrogant attitudes, being rude, best of all selfishness. So our good person the one who lives deep down in us knows all those behaviors are not great, but they are not that bad. So we continue to justify all the reasons not to change.

Once you start disseminating them and working on removing those traits, you will see the war that your flesh will create, because it does not want to lose it's rights. Your flesh has been in control for years getting everything it want's.

This is our spiritual work. To begin to peel the onion of false ideologies and habits that has become our boring unfulfilled lives. Well today is a new day, and it is more than ok for you to say enough is enough, things are going to change around here.

The Power Of Your Words

Oh that tongue of ours, it can get us in such hot water like nothing I have ever seen. I have been the giver of its vileness and the receiver.

The bible clearly states "By your words are you justified "I have learned that firsthand, once it leaves your lips there is no taking back! I don't care what the other person says about forgiving you etc. . . . They will never forget!

So with that being said I stop and think now before speaking. The hard part is in learning restriction to withdraw in the middle of a serious heated confrontation. If you could achieve this one thing and return with having had time to contemplate and reflect on how the matter should be handled you will change the course of your life in ways that are beyond measure.

Something I practice daily is do not engage with people exuding a bad aura, to put it mildly. Your love meter will be tested greatly on this matter especially if this is a button pusher for you. Walk the talk of Love and it will prevail and pray, pray, pray. . . .This is a perfect time to call in your team angels to help with the situation. You can practice this ahead of time also with upcoming events of stress or deadlines.

Power Of Your Thoughts

Oh Yes, your thoughts do count. Remember the three, spirit, soul and body. Well, they all have a mind of their own. Daily these three are competing for your attention. Problem today is no one knows which one to listen too or you have been taught to listen to the wrong one.

Your spirit should be ruler of your life; in this your intuition will flourish or the "still small voice". Upon your knowledge of this and practicing this path you can only make the very best decisions about everything that is right for you.

You must separate yourself from the minds concepts which choose to be about all of the lusts and gratifications of the flesh only. Walking in the spirit can only be of love and giving love. This takes a very conscious decision to follow this path. It goes against everything you believe and takes pure faith to follow.

But the rewards are endless. You will awaken to a self you did not even know existed, so, then your true life's purpose and contentment reveals all the great things that have been inside of you.

Are you ready to start peeling back that onion of your

soul to find this true self? We all hear it calling us at some point in our lives and it has many voices and tones and levels of volume.

Do you want to hear, sounds so cliché but, the truth will set you free. What is that kind of freedom worth to you? I had no choice but, to listen because my soul was aching for its release. Once I started this journey I could easily see I would never turn back nor did I want to.

Find your excitement, listen to your haunches guiding you to try something different or find out about something new. Go investigate all the different kinds of faith and spirituality there is and follow your heart to the one that resonates with your soul. God is so good and will help you every step of the way.

We are not expected to conform to anyone's confines of any religion. You are to seek and have your true relationship with God that is as unique as you are. No one's journey is the same; everybody has different classes to take to get to the destiny of their own personal fulfillment. That is why there are so many choices, if you think about it, God thought of everything already.

Stop letting your flesh talk you out of doing another thing in your life that could bring you a joy that you never knew before. Stop listening to the lies swirling around in your head. Learn to change your mind set too one of success and accomplishment. Allow your soul to heal from its wounds and allow your spirit to then lead you to a life of Love and great joy and find a new dream. So where do we go from here?

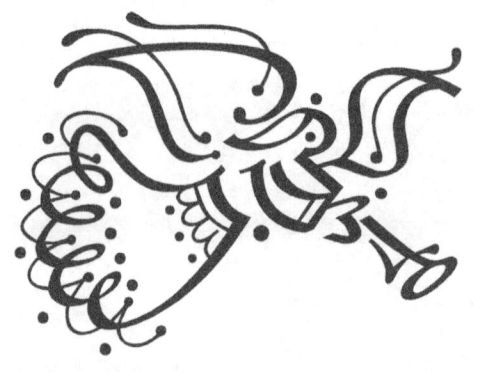

So let's Meet Some Angels

My personal favorite is <u>**Arch Angel Michael**</u>. Well as bold as the title is the commander of all the angels. He is our entrance and guardian of our heaven. He helps our guardian angels he leads all the other angels to carry out all the issues of God.

He is great encourager because of his strength and fierce courage as well as protection. When you have connected with Michael you have no fear of anything for his is fearless and is always ready to help. Do not hesitate to call on him for overcoming fear and strength. He helps all who are seeking their life's purpose.

My second favorite is <u>**Archangel Raphael.**</u> He is the great healer and comforter of all sickness and torment of any kind. Call on him immediately when any type of illness or sickness is attempting to attach itself to you or has come upon you. He will see you through all of it from the beginning to the end.

My third favorite is <u>**Archangel Jophiel.**</u> Jophiel helps me tremendously for the inspiration and beautification of our surrounding environment. As well with my own personal beauty appreciation. Seek Jophiel for peace and calmness after a lot of business demands and deadlines. He will help you to slow down and have calm thoughts and reflect upon thoughts of beauty and love.

My fourth favorite **Archangel is Metatron.** It is said he once walked the earth and was transformed to his status of an Archangel. This being said I relate to him because he shows us that we all are capable of transformation and resurrection. I see in him the fact that there is no death. He lived a human life and resurrected as an angel. Metatron is a great protector of children. He also guides our spiritual understanding.

These are just four of the many angels in existence. God loves us so much we have so many Angels just waiting to do our bidding. But how do we connect, and like me I am sure you are asking and why would they do anything for me?

Because God is Awesome, and he did think of everything regarding your wellbeing and what it would take for you to accomplish that which you are here to do.

Your birth is no accident, your being here is no mistake. From a totally physical flesh level with a poor mind set, that is what you would believe and every person that speaks that nonsense to you has taken a foot hold in your mind. The good news is you do not have to listen to that broken boring replay in your head anymore.

It's Time To Take Back What is Rightfully Yours!

You're Spirit, mind and control over your body. We are not going to let anyone steal our peace, joy, abundance and the truth to live the life that is waiting for us......

Ok so how did that feel, is it starting to rise up in you that you can do this or is your mind still talking down to you. Please recite these words whenever you feel this mindset coming over you. "I have everything I need inside of me and I am Perfect"

Please continue to say this to yourself until you really believe it. Then move on to the next affirmation for the place you are at on your journey. You can apply this method to any type of situation you are facing. Also call on your angels for support and protection. Don't forget the trick with Angels is you have to ask for help they will not interfere without your permission.

Picture a line up if you will of all your angels standing behind you, only problem is that they all have their hands handcuffed behind their backs, just waiting for you to speak words of faith so they can go to work on your behalf. The minute you release words of faith they jump into action. When you speak words of defeat you have put them back in jail waiting to get out again.

And I know you are thinking how that can be so? Angels are all power full and mighty. Key is only when you release them to be, that is the way the Creator set it up. That is a universal law. It is what it is....Learn the system....Walk in victory....

Remember how we spoke about not knowing everything, just go with it. Do not believe me try it for yourself. Then tell me all about it. I know your story will be one of success.

Why Prayer

We all believe in something, what is that you believe in? Everyone pretty much believes in one true source of power. We just have different names for it. But, it stands to reason most of us do know what prayer is and why it is beneficial.

One, you have to believe there is more to this world then what you see of it and what you are experiencing of it. So that being said are you interested in the rest of it. Where is all the different places and lifetimes you could have already experienced. Find out about your past, and I mean many pasts. There is so much more to you and your existence stop limiting yourself to your limited mind. If you are willing to just open yourself up to a possibility and go with it you may be very surprised on where you end up.

I have found out so many things about my past that I truly understand why and who I am now. Long time ago I would have doubted this. I have learned to check things out then make an informed decision. If you don't like it dismiss it, if it resonates with you run with it. Find out all you can take what you need of it and throw away the rest. Then go on to the next subject. Let's all be like little children again and ask "Why" and find out "Why".

Prayer is the ultimate release for the soul; it is the hotline to the main line GOD. The creator loves to hear from us, because he loves his kids, just like we love our kids. And just like any parent we want to be proud of our kids and we want our kids to behave and we also want to give our kids everything that they desire. So why do we all think when it comes to God, that is not true?

Another lie of the Mind Set. It really is that simple. We have been conditioned and trained to believe these lies. But, it's time we stand up and say no more. I am going to be brave go out and face my fear and retrain my thoughts because I have the right (Choice) to do so!

Are you excited yet, I am jumping out of my seat right now. You know why because as I keep saying God is Awesome. . .and he welcomes the challenge to prove himself to you, all you have to do is act in faith. Now let's be real here. You are going to have to take the necessary steps of change and commitment to follow the methods of the universal laws. None of this is just going to fall upon you and poof done.

It takes a true desire and intent to make this happen, but it will happen and you can stand back and watch with Amazement. If then you are like me; I stand back daily and I cannot even put into words the changes, blessings that have come to me. . . . WOW.

I would not ask you to do something that does not work, it is through my own discovery and my angels pushing me that I am sharing this with you now. . . .

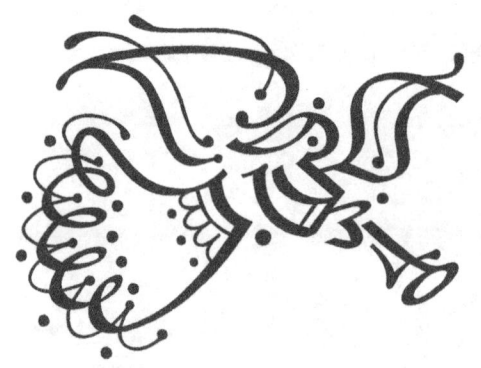

How Am I Going to Change I Have Tried?

Remember how we spoke about words, tried is one of those horrible endless failure words. Never use it again. Please remove this word from your vocabulary. When this word is spoken you have already attached a failure to what you are declaring. Jesus said "by your words you are justified."

That means good or bad there it is you said it. So let's get really deep here. Think about all the things you say daily that keep you where you are.

Here is a small list that we all take for granted, myself included. All that is required is to retrain that brain!

a) I'll never have anything
b) I am so ugly
c) I'll never be rich

d) I'll never finish school
e) I'll never get out of this neighborhood
f) I'll never get to go to college

g) I'll never get off drugs
h) I'll never get married
i) I'll never have my own business

j) I tried I just can't do it

k) I'll never own my own home

See what I mean, now replace I'LL never with I've tried. Same affect, same result, failure. That is a universal law you asked for it and it responded. Get what I am saying now, you can think and speak your way out of anything.

Now do not blow that out of context, your efforts moving in the correct direction will also affect the outcome. But your faith and action is what puts, everything into action in heaven and on earth.

Why Jesus

I keep referring to Jesus because I finally get what he was trying to say. So some food for thought for you I have listed several versus with locations and let's see if it stirs anything up in you. The words are so powerful to me now. I myself am guilty of taking its power for granted. Please use any of the Verses below for affirmations they are mighty. I also encourage you to make up your own.

My personal daily affirmation:

"I am so happy and grateful that money and health comes to me now through multiple sources on a continual basis for the sake of sharing. . .I appreciate everyday as an opportunity for the universe to manifest these things in my life. Focusing on the intent and renewing of my mind. . .I will no longer believe in the old ways of conditioning and will retrain my thoughts to the universal law of abundance that is available to everyone"

Please write your own that inspires you or that which comes from your soul.

Some suggested affirmations regarding different situations:

Amplified Bible

II Corinthians 7:1

Therefore, since these great promises are ours, beloved, let us cleanse ourselves from everything that contaminates and defiles the body and spirit, and bring our consecration to completeness in the reverential fear of God.

Love that verse as I said earlier remember how the body and mind control the spirit, here you can clearly see that God wants us to change, renew our spirit and mind and body to completeness (resurrection) back to God, get it?

Psalm 16:9

Therefore my heart is glad and my glory (my inner self) rejoices; my body to shall rest and confidently dwell in safety.

Psalm 16:11

You will show me the path of life; in your presence is fullness of joy, at your right hand there are pleasures forevermore.

Psalm 62:7

With God rests my salvation and my glory; he is my Rock of unyielding strength and impenetrable hardness, and my refuge is in God!

You worked up yet, couple more for you.

Psalm 66:19-20

19) But certainly God has heard me; He has given heed to the voice of my prayer

20) Blessed be God, who has not rejected my prayer nor removed his mercy and loving-kindness from being (as it always is) with me.

Matthew 5:8

Blessed (happy, enviably fortunate, and spiritually prosperous-possessing the "happiness produced by the Experience of God's favor and especially conditioned by the revelation of his grace. Regardless of their outward conditions) are the pure in heart, for they shall see God!

That is just some, there are many more and from many different sources. Again find that which inspires you and go for it. Stop telling you inner voice to be quite. Your spirit has so much to show you if you would just slow down breath and listen. All that stuff in the world will never buy you the peace you are looking for. Stop trusting the world with your life, turn back to the source.

Appreciation and Gratitude

What are you thankful for? Do you really know? Daily we take for granted little things that really make our life great. You should be able to give sometime everyday just telling the creator what you are grateful for. Yes we have needs and we should ask and pray for them as well. But, I truly believe if we cannot appreciate what we have why would we appreciate more. We cannot allow our hearts to become hard and cold with the entitlement syndrome that seems to running rampant these days.

We are all so busy chasing this elusive dream of success that we lose the day to day joy that is given in each moment. I can tell you that as I look back on my life and my achievements it was the journey that was the best part. Once we reach our goal it never really stacks up to the image we had in our mind. We have to stop and remember that today might be our last, as horrible as that sounds but, are your affairs really in order. If your life were to end right now, are your good with everyone in your life that is important to you? Have you told the people that are in your life how much you love them and appreciate them?

See if we can't do that, how could we expect more. We

must appreciate what we have? Now saying that, you can also find out what you do not need in your life anymore as well.

This is where Love comes into play because it will discern all that is good from that which goes against it. The two cannot dwell together. With love comes unity. Hate creates chaos.

These two opposites can never occupy the same space. Plainly said it is impossible to please God without Love. God is Love. He wants you to express yourself in love so he can express his love to you. When we go beyond ourselves and love others as ourselves we are revealing the God within us in his image. So as a great parent does he can only reward his children for their great works.

Are we there yet?

That is the question that burns inside of all of us, hurry, hurry and hurry some more. We need to slow down and enjoy the journey. Does it really matter how long it takes to get there as long as we get there.

This earthy life you are now living is one big school for the elevation of your soul. Find time to absorb that which you are learning and sharpen your spiritual skills. When you start this journey you will find all your intuitive skills will heighten and your internal guide will be clearer and louder to you.

This will assist you in your everyday work and in pursuing that which really is the desire of your heart.

What Are You Chasing After?

What are you chasing after? Will this bring ever lasting peace and goodwill into your life? What purpose will it serve to humanity as a whole? All great ideas are born on this premise.

Discovering your true dream will also define its existence. In other words this will be the foundation of its greatness.

All great ideas are born in heaven first, and then manifested on earth. We are created to create just like the Creator!

Play on words there but, true no less. We are all artist here painting a picture. What does your painting look like? When you look at your canvas are you inspired or bored or worse see nothing?

You can change this. You just need to take that first leap of faith and start with baby steps. Try this as an action plan, buy a paint brush and everyday look at it and declare, "I will add a new stroke to my canvas today". Start visualizing the canvas with a new picture of what your new reality is going to be. Keep moving forward till that vision is what your eyes see materialize in this earthy plain.

As you practice this and reach your inspired vision, you can move onto the next one and on and on it begins. You are now walking in your new painted canvas.

Faith is the absence of things not yet seen. Believe do not doubt in your heart that what your mind perceives and your mouth speaks in the result of your faith turned into manifestation.

These are the things that God responds too; words of faith and belief are what your angels can act on. Stop defeating yourself. Release your faith and see where it can lead you.

You can retrain your brain! Only you can stop the chatter that is taking place in your head. Start to rewrite the script that keeps playing over and over to one that screams of joy, happiness and success. You will never overcome the negative till you replace it with a positive affirmation. Yes I know you have heard it all before. So, how is the the script that is playing now working for you. You would have never picked this up to read if something down deep inside of you was not screaming "I can't take this anymore, there has to be a better way".…..

Yes something that sounds so simple is mightier than you think. But, do not believe me. Take the step make the effort, then stand back and watch the magic begin. Your thoughts are as powerful as your words. What is in your heart needs to rise up to meet the brain. Stop letting your circumstances keep you from doing what will only change your life for the better.

How would you like to dream again? Does saying "I can" even interest you? Does that sound like a possibility only for everyone else, not you?

So What about Love

Back to basics. Let's review the scripture one more time with more explanation on why. We are all created out of love and our most inherent nature in us all is to be loved. So why do we not act that way. Because this is earth school, we need to learn how and why and when to use this great love that dwells in every human on this planet. There are no exceptions to this rule. Only our ego that rages constantly with our spirit man for dominion over us.....free will has the right to choose.

1 Corinthians 13:4-7 (Amplified Bible)
Verse 4
Love endures long and is patient and kind

So how are you with this one, this will be a challenge for everyone always. We are human and as long as all of us are living together on this planet, we will be tested from time to time.

Practice does make perfect and you will find that it takes longer for someone to get under your skin and you'll recognize the challenge when it happens.

Love never is envious nor boils over with jealousy, is not boastful or vainglorious, does not display itself haughtily.

WAKE UP AND LIVE IN LOVE

Jealousy, envy there's a real tough one, our world is spinning so fast and we are constantly being bombarded with stuff to buy and what to wear and where to live so that other people will be envious of us and what we have.

Just saying; you see where this endless suffocating loveless behavior will take you. I would rather be in love with my God and family and friends and live a full filled life then one of chasing the endless dream that is so elusive. "Just" an illusion. Why not create something with some substance.

Please do not think I am condemning having beautiful things etc. I believe God created them all for our enjoyment. But, you must keep God first so the things; do not get a hold on you, lest you forget where they came from to begin with.

It is not conceited (arrogant and inflated with pride): it is not rude unmannerly) and does not act unbecomingly.

Now this one is a real heart breaker, we all have fallen short in being rude or arrogant at the most inopportune times. This is when our patience is tested to see what the response will be. So patience starts things going and our response determines the outcome. Are we going to act in a kind manner? Or be rude and prideful with the only thought being I am right and no matter what I am going to Win!

When a situation has come to this point, you can see where the only concern is you. . .that is pride. I know; I do not like that but, that is the truth of the mater. When you remove yourself from the situation and act in a loving manner with your concern only being for the other person, removing all of the negative behavior from the situation. You then allow Love to enter into the situation and change the outcome for everyone.

No matter what; it takes "Two to Tango" with any problem that arises. Again, do not allow someone else to dictate your behavior because, then you can truly say you are only a puppet. When we look at the event in that way, it can take on a completely different effect. Then you become the puppet master.

Love (God's love in us) does not insist on its own rights or its own way, for it is not self-seeking: it is not touchy or fretful or resentful: it takes no account of the evil done to it (it pays no attention to the suffered wrong).

This is where are hard work begins. By faith is the love of God in us but, we must activate its use. There is no magic wand here. The magic is that everything you need has been instilled in you from birth. Our work begins when we start to search to find our true self and sort through all the ego based actions to reveal the true self (which is of Love) and then show it, live it, as well as feel it.

There is no place for ego at this stage. When we surrender to the love that is already present and let it flow we then can change the circumstance of our lives in every situation. Nothing will appear as it was once to you. When you step over to the commitment of a love base life you will find that you will automatically have no desire for the things that were once your triggers for anger, you self- loathing, or fear based reactive behavior.

You will basically get you off your mind, so that love can flow through you and out to others. In return your needs will be met, you will have fullness of joy in your life, and you will be loved by others.

It does not rejoice at injustice and unrighteousness, but rejoices when right and truth prevail. Love bears up under anything and everything that comes is ever ready to believe the best of every person. Its hopes are fadeless under all circumstances, and it endures everything (without weakening).

So there you have it, reverts back to faith that all is under control and will be handled in trust of love and that even justice will prevail when it looks like it will not. Love is strong and never backs down. It is what keeps us sane sort to speak. This is the element that rocks us to the core of our being and will make all of us go to great lengths to have it.

What would you do to keep it? Knowing that, it changes everything in your life so it works for your benefit and all who come in contact with you.

It is contagious, once you operate in this consciousness you will never want to return to one of confusion or chaos. Our egos want to keep busy with us, there is no time to do anything else or think about anyone else. We will go to great lengths to schedule and plan all of our days with a very me based mentality.

When is the last time you performed a truly random act of kindness? When you walk in love, your day will not be Satisfactory unless you have performed several through-out the day.

Love never fails (never fades out or becomes obsolete or comes to an end).

This is what the creator wants you to know above all else. He will never change he is a constant today and forever. In this your heart should be confident that all is well on planet earth and your being here now is very important.

Our lives are not random happenings of nothingness. We have to get rid of fear based rejection that creeps into our souls creating a death of sorts right here on earth.

We came here to live and help and love each other, as well as learn the lessons our soul desires to elevate us on our spiritual journey.

Our ego is the part of the game we all cannot seem to remember or get rid of. It was all part of the plan for you to achieve your highest spiritual goals.

My perception of hell is here; on earth as is the choice to live in a state of heaven. Your choice for a life of Love or one that is crazy and chaotic.

We all have to stop entertaining this hateful spirit of lack, sickness, disease. Start perceiving yourself as well, rich and physically empowered to do whatever you need to do to live your life's potential.

I Have Heard it All Before

Yes we have all heard something along these lines before. But, how are you feeling about it inside? Is your spirit finally motivated to change or just continue on the same path to nowhere with the same feelings of guilt, shame and condemnation.

You will know when you have had enough, I care and I have been there. I personally do not want anyone to feel the darkness and loneness that comes with these feelings.

When you begin to learn that feelings are ego driven and not heart and soul driven you can change the situation then manifest the outcome that is the desire of your heart.

Your life's purpose is deep within you. We all have it there we designed it very carefully before beginning our human tour on this earth. Remember we are all just visiting. We have invited many other people to share and help us along our path to greatness (if we choose it). There are no robots here. Only you can choose.

God is so merciful that if you get it wrong you get to do it again, till you get it right. So stop fearing a God you might feel is out to get you or against you. This is not in any of Gods, words or actions. He is Love; only ego can create those feelings of negativity. Again it's about choices.

We make millions of them every day. From the moment we get up in the morning till we go to bed at night. Sometimes you don't even sleep because you have choices rolling around in your head on what to do next.

Let's Take A Survey

Stop reading and for the next 5 minutes write down on a piece of paper 5 things you dislike about yourself and 5 things you like the most about you. When you are done, put your list aside and save it for later. Oh by the way please write the date at the top.

How easy or hard was that for you? If you like to journal please write how your feeling right now from doing that and any emotions this has stirred up in you. Better yet did you learn something new about yourself?

We will go back to this list later and will review how to make your plan to change today to a new tomorrow.

So Who Is This God?

Well before I begin this part, work on imagining that you have never heard of "God". Now I will describe all that he is and you can see if any of the descriptions listed match any event or thoughts or knowing's (intuition) about God.

God is Love, gentle, parental, wise, protective, giving, merciful, playful, funny, creative, cool, non- judgmental, peaceful, Good. . . . .

Sound like anybody you know? God is all that we should be aspiring too, that is it. Only difference is he has mastered all of the above and more. We are works in progress.

The funny part about it is you came here with that very intention. But, because God is so wise, the memory of it is removed and your soul is allowed to remember in slow increments sort to speak or specifically scheduled downloads of this prior information to help you. Why because you would freak out. . . some of you are thinking this is far out. But, take it in. As I said before keep an open heart, allow you heart and soul to ponder on these thoughts, not your mind (ego).

Learn to trust your heart, that is where you're most

creative and aspiring ideas straight from heaven will be downloaded and will be spoken to you through sudden thoughts or gut feelings or deep intuitive nudges. Stop, listen, discern.

Calling all Angels

Not comfortable using your intuitive skills or listening to the still small voice. Call on your Angels to assist you in how to strengthen these skills. We all have them, but like a muscle they have to be used and maintained. Once you become comfortable using this skill you will have no doubts about your decisions and what is next in your life for you. It will also protect you from danger. Prayer and meditation are great for honing in on these skills.

But get used to hearing the stillness which will impart to you answers for all things beyond your wildest dreams. This is no fantasy although sometimes as I have often felt how surreal it can be. Enjoy it, bask in every lovely minute. This rea-firms that we are connected to the spiritual and the physical plane all at the same time. Once you have really ingested this you can live the life you were created to live.

Your dream can become your true reality with all the aspirations you thought would never be a part of your life. Remember that movie I spoke about. Well now is your chance to rewrite the new version of you. Be bold think big, expand your vision. Like the renewing of your mind you have to retrain the brain from thinking small to thinking big.

You must believe that nothing and I mean nothing is IMPOSSIBLE!

No room for wishful thinking. This has to become your new way of life so that every thought and every word is infused with your new life with all of your new dreams and new desires that will not only inspire you but, will become contagious to everyone around you.

People will want to know what has gotten in to you. So get ready to tell your story.

It's Too Late For Me

Stop saying that and don't even give that thought any place in your head anymore. That is a lie from the ego. Remember the ego wants to keep you down and unsuccessful and timid and unsure of everything you are and could possibly become.

This is the part that makes the transformation so sweet. You do not have to stay that way and you can choose to change it.

When you make a heartfelt promise to yourself that today is a new day, nothing on this earth can stop you.

Activate your faith and the creator will take care of the rest. You were born to succeed. You do not have to be another tragic story.

Your greatness has so many sides to it, like the onion you start to peel each layer off and explore the next level of you without fear, do it in love. You may even find some things out about yourself you didn't even know existed.

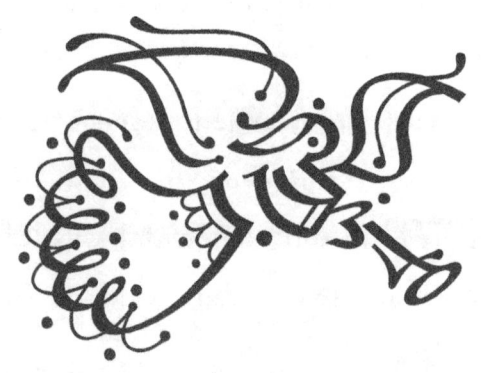

I Am Afraid

Well get in line, we all are. Only difference is the level of fears we all have. But, the only way to overcome is to dive in head on and address that which causes you to hold back all that you can become.

Remember the feeling of fear is not the issue, it is the fear that e-mobilizes you into a state of non-action.

Sometimes just acknowledging the fear is enough to erase it from your path. Now I am not suggesting you go out and do anything high risk or life threatening. This is not the kind of fear we are speaking of. What I am referring to is the fear of let's say meeting new people, or just being able to tell someone you really care about how you love them and appreciated them. Doing an act of kindness for a perfect stranger. Trying a new art like dancing or painting etc. You get what I am saying the thing that you tell yourself you are no good at.

Find Your Inner Child

$\mathcal{I}$ am sure at one time or another you have recalled memories of your childhood that you remember to be carefree and happy beyond measure. No fear, No Stress, No Pain, - superior feeling of indestructible....not even the fear of death.

What happened? We became adults and everything got harder and we became cynical and self-loathing.

How boring is that? I don't know about you but, I dreamed a lot as a child and miss that limitless possibility I felt.

Part of our re-birth so to speak is to recapture the lost part of our youth that we tucked away once we became grown-ups.

I have learned that person still exists very much deep down inside of us, that is our pure true self. That part never left, we just put it away.

When you begin your journey, this child like self will re-emerge with your new grown-up image. Yes they can become one whole person. You will no longer separate the two they will re-connect back into one as was the way you were created to begin with.

This Is Just Too Hard!

You cannot afford to put this off any longer. Stop putting your life off because you are listening to your ego again telling you, who do you think you are? You will never accomplish this; you are setting yourself up to fail again. We do not listen to that voice anymore. Start telling yourself how great you are and something wonderful is waiting for you and I will never give up because God loves me, and I love me too.

Keep saying it till you believe. If you have to repeat it hundred times per day, keep at it, till it sticks. You will notice one day you won't say it anymore because you just finally believe it to be true, and that my friend is the truth.

Don't Forget To Pray

Prayer should be informal and a very personal conversation that for my self goes on all day with the Creator God.

My life is from him and I give it back to him. So for that reason I could not imagine not having God in every second of my life.

This is the hard lesson I learned. I tried it all by myself. It did not work. I let my Ego run the whole show for so long and after my continued repeat failures the only choice was to surrender and open my-self up to something that went beyond my little space of existence.

Oh yeah that hurt like hell, but then hell was the chaos I was living. So my only choice was to surrender to the force of Love that heals all. So with great patience and a slow steady action plan I have overcome that which once was my death sentence.

I now have my joy back. I love things I never loved before. I see people in a completely different light. We are all doing the same thing. Trying to find our way and just wanting to be loved.

But, now I truly care about other people. My life is

no longer just my little circle of being. We are all in this together. Yes everything I do affects _everything!_

When you start looking at your actions, thoughts and how they impact us all in the collective consciousness. You cannot go back to being on a self-level only.

Once you have felt the true essence and depth of love from the creator. You then know how it must be shared with everyone.

You then begin to imagine your new transformation of an ego based self to a love based self. This desire will rise up in you like an ocean and ebb and flow till you have put all that it requires into it to become the awesome vision that you can see peeking out over on the other side.

Wanting and desiring nothing more than to see the manifestation of this dream become the reality on this plane. This should be your desire and with this new found dream comes the joy, love and reward for you. A journey that no words can ever be enough to describe the depth of its bounty.

You can say goodbye to your hell of chaos and start living the life that God the Creator intended for you to live. One of great health, abundance and lacking nothing.

That Sounds too Good to be True

As I said earlier, please do not take my word for it. Try it, it has to work, it is how the universe works. This Law is for everyone. No one with a sincere heart can fail, impossible. The only failure is doubt and unbelief.

If you say, act and believe, the lies have to back out of the way and clear out. You have given your Angel's permission to act on your behalf. You do your part and God and the Angels will do theirs. It is really that Simple.

As Jesus himself said "Ask and it shall be given, knock and it shall be opened". Now don't go and make that simple statement complicated we have done that enough over the years. Jesus really did mean it to be that simple.

Learn From The Example

Jesus came so that we would have life and have it more abundantly. Do you understand that statement? Jesus is our example of what we should aspire to and that with true surrender of self you can master your life living in a state of abundance and peace in love, while going about and doing good and loving others unconditionally all things will be added unto you so that your life is not only fulfilled but, you live lacking nothing and wanting nothing. Wow, can you grasp the enormity of that? Still telling yourself that is too good to be true? This is where you have to start renewing your mind and that "I can "and "I will "live in this true state of fulfillment. Because "I am "in the image of the Creator.

The Beauty of Your Soul

Inside of you is your true essence challenging you to release it. Some of us have found it before others, while some of us seem to struggle endlessly to find that special place deep within. God has always seen you as perfect you only have to convince yourself that you are. Everything you would ever need in this life is buried deep inside of you. The only thing you need to do is give it permission to express itself. Once you start on your journey of self-discovery you will slowly and methodically start peeling every layer of your ego away to reach down deep within the part of you where your soul can start to sing. This may sound hooky and so woo woo. But, I can only stress it is a very eye opening journey that cannot be rushed and believe it or not with every new discovery of your true self, you will stand back in amazement thinking I did not know I could do that or can do that. You will learn about your inner self and how truly different it can and is from your outer self. You will begin to see yourself in a whole new "Light".

Change Your View

You have heard that old cliché many times keep doing the same thing again and again expecting a different result. Stop it already; you are never going to get a different result till you start doing something differently. Yes I know we don't like change, change is uncomfortable. But guess what? Only change can bring you the desired results you want to achieve.

Yes you heard me correctly you are going to have to do something completely out of your comfort zone to get on the path to success.

You start with baby steps and prioritize what your immediate desire of intention is at this very moment. Doing this not only gives you breathing room but, allows you to gently ease yourself into the desired result. This process cannot be hurried for in that comes sloppy-ness and lack of true intention will only lead to a false sense of mastery that was never achieved.

The goal here is to start on a path that not only gives true inner happiness and fulfillment but, will also manifest on your outer self because light can only shine. You will not be able to contain your new inner release of self. All will notice.

That is the way the Creator intended it to be. We only have to follow the example. Use any method you choose as long as the goal above all else is to love one another as we love ourselves, and treat everyone with human dignity; and love the lord your God with all you heart and soul.

If you Need Religion

There are a multitude of choices when it comes to which practice of faith and or traditional or non-traditional religion you want to participate in. There are many choices because life is about choices and we need different choices to help us with our needs.

I personally have studied 2-3 different types of religions and have come to the conclusion that I like many characteristics of all three and cannot stuff my beliefs into one type only.

I feel very blessed that I can in this great country of ours do that kind of study and have free choice to then decide how I want to express and or live out the faith that I believe in.

The point I am trying to make is that Faith as I call it, is the only type of spiritual study that is necessary. Study your interest and then try out that way of practice and see what works for you. The great illusion is that faith without works is dead. Ever hear that before? So as mentioned earlier the power backing the intent is what brings about the final desired result.

This is where your belief of love plays a significant role in all of your decisions and thoughts so you can manifest that which you desire without any weakness or fear. Always expecting nothing but, the best from the Creator. I am proud to say that my "Father "is **Awesome!**

As you do your studies you will learn what your motivators are, your strengths and weaknesses. This is not to make you miserable but, to help you get to the elevation and growth of your soul. Only your spirit knows your true desire of growth and what it will take to get there. Learning to Love yourself even more through this process will bring forth that true self you have never met.

Like the onion I spoke of before, you will find this to be enlightening and very eye opening.

Trusting Someone Other Than yourself

So where does the Creator and or God, which ever name you use; fit into your life. This is where it gets complicated if you are a control freak or a slider as I call it. If you constantly feel that you cannot remove yourself from any situation without being the chief organizer or worse never acting on anything because you rather not have to make any decisions. This is where I am reminded of what Jesus said about being Luke warm. No fence riding. Make a firm decision and go with it, using your intuition the way God intended it to be.

I can only say again as a reminder, you have everything you need already inside of you. You only have to start digging to uncover all the wonderful mysteries of you.

Remaining in fear will continue to only keep you from all that is waiting for you. I am reminded of always keeping your peace about any given situation. Learning to not only create peace in your life but, maintaining it as well. This is just one of the many gifts already instilled in you. You just have to read the owner's manual.

Re-train That Brain

Yes you will literally have to retrain all your old mental linguistics.....Stop playing that old recording over and over in your head. Find a new speech and memorize it...

I cannot stress enough the importance of the chatter that goes on in your head and how it affects literally every part of your life from you wealth to health and career. This is no joke and no laughing matter. This is the root cause of why you are where and how you are today.

I spoke earlier about rewriting that movie in your head. Start dreaming and visualizing the new movie that is going to take place. Now you just can't do it for a couple of times and that is the magic answer. This is a true way of life from driving to work to taking a shower, doing the dishes. What is playing in your head at all times (Yes it all counts).

Once you grasp this concept and start changing, with that will come the results and you will be amazed. You will never go back to your old ways again. But, this must be done faithfully and with great dedication. Remember you are trying to re-train a 20, 35, 42, 55, 65+ brain. The longer you have been the old way the more determined you have to be to stick with it and keep at it, till one day you will notice that the old thought pattern is just a very distant memory. You will adjust very quickly to this new mind set because as you begin events and circumstances will begin to change and you will be able to see the living proof of your thoughts coming to pass right before your eyes. This will in-turn elevates your faith, raise your soul up to the next level and inspire you to do things you never thought possible.

Growing Pains

Journaling is a great way to track your progress and growth changes as you start to apply some of these methods in your life. Remember to be kind to yourself and do it from a place of Love not guilt or condemnation or worse fear!

We can no longer hold on to the what if's and maybe's. Stop riding the invisible fence of indecision. Enough of life has passed a lot of us by to give one more minute to confusion or continuing in lack of anything from career to relationships to our ultimate life's purpose.

None of this will disappear overnight; it took a lot longer to create. But, you will see tremendous progress and even miracles as you progress. So more than anything do not give up. When you begin on this journey you will discover that it will continue on for the rest of your life. It will open your heart up to so many wonderful opportunities that you know it is going to take the rest of your life to complete your new hearts desires.

God will take you through from glory to glory. You will look back along the way and wonder how did I ever settle for anything less.

Never say Never

One thing I have learned over the years is that desires can be very powerful and backed with intention the universe is there ready to respond. So the old adage "be careful what you ask for you just might get it" is so true. Even on the things you do not want. Be mindful of your thoughts and intentions when you are trying to manifest your desires. Really take time to search and pray about what is really in your heart. Once you have done this you can make a plan with your angels and guardian angel with the love of God to bring that which you most desire into fruition.

It is liken to when the planets are perfectly lined up that we have the best show in the evening sky. The same with your life and events just flowing as they should be because you and your angels are in alignment with the assistance of the Creator to help and guide you to accomplish that which only you were sent to do. No one else can do this for you or in the manner you would do it.

You Are One Of A Kind

As you go on your journey you will have times of doubt and attempts that seem as failures. I have been told the more you are doubting and or feeling fear or angst, this should inspire you even more, meaning the world is shaking because of your awesome power and knows the potential of what you have to offer. I know in the midst of this, these words sound eloquent and pretty but, that does not help the sick butterfly stomach wreaking havoc on our body in that moment.

Yes back to a spirit being have a real human experience. Sometimes it is too human. Feelings of disconnect can make you question all of your intentions and desires if they are truly in alignment with the Creator God.

This is your ego's last ditch effort to keep you in the familiar bondage you have grown accustomed to.

Remember what we said about ego, there is no room for God when the ego is on the scene. Love will also take a back seat to this foe whenever it rears its ugly head.

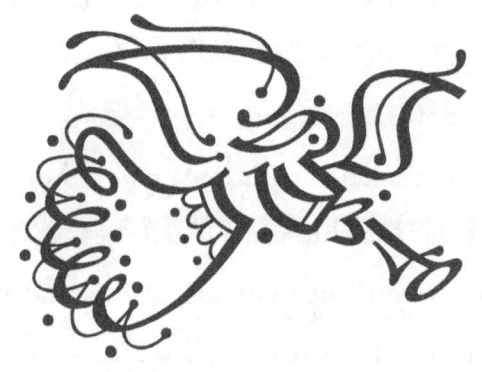

Why Declare

Words are very powerful, when thought out and delivered with the power of its intent with a goal, there is nothing that can stop us from accomplishing what we desire to do. (As long as it is done in Love to benefit and never harm another) success is assured.

Below I have listed a few small short prayers to invoke assistance from our angels and God. Please feel free to create your own; they should be words from your heart. Keep it short and direct.

* May all of my communications be clear and full of Love.
* May I be a messenger of Divine Love every day in my Life.
* May I have the patience to listen and understand.

These are more on communication skills in relation to the Arch Angel Gabriel, who assists us in speaking our truth.

You select the Angel that you would like to work with on your particular issue that you want to address first.

Ahead I will give you some definitions of some of the Arch Angels that are more commonly associated with our day to day lives. If you find one particular angel resonates with you more that another or that you feel more than one appeals to you, please open yourself up to them they are all here to help and assist us in any way possible. Again do not forget, they need our permission to help us in our lives. Remember invite them to come and be present with you and help you.

The Arch Angels

* Michael

Helps us to follow our truth without compromising our integrity and helps us to find our true natures and be faithful to who we really are. Protection.

* Gabriel

If you wish to receive visions of angelic guidance regarding the direction you are going in. Assists in communications and helping overcome fear and procrastination.

* Haniel

Help with speaking in public and bringing beauty, harmony and loving friends into your life. Seek guidance on crystal and potion remedies for healing.

* Jophiel

Patron of artists, helping with artistic projects, thinking beautiful thoughts, to see and appreciate beauty around us. He illuminates our creative spark by giving us ideas and energy to carry out artistic ventures.

* Metaron

He is the keeper of the "Book of Life" of all akashic records. He is the chief recorder in Heaven and in charge of recording and organizing all the records. He helps us understand Heaven's perspective and to learn how to work with the Angelic realm.

* Uriel

Expertise is divine magic, problem solving, spiritual understanding, studies, alchemy, weather, earth changes and writing. Considered to be the Archangel to heal recovery in the aftermath of natural disasters.

* Sandalphon

Chief role is to carry human prayers to God so they may be answered. Keeper of music that inspires and heals.

* Raphael

The master in healing of all humans and animals. He helps to heal the spirit, body and the soul if called upon.

* Zadkiel

Divine comforter that bestows wisdom, allowing clear vision to take place over the obstacles that limit us from enjoying true spiritual fulfillment.

* Shamael

The lifter of great sorrows and finding love in our heart. He works with us to build strong foundations for relationships, careers to be long lasting.

These are just a few of the angels available to us for support in all the aspects of our lives as we transition through our life journey. Call upon the angel needed for the part of your life that you are currently facing. This is their greatest joy, to receive consent from you to assist you with your needs. You are not putting them out, nor are they too busy to help you with whatever ails you. "Ask and it shall be given".

Take the Time

It is a learned thing that takes practice that is to take time to be quite and listen to the inner being of your voice that beckons you to listen. This still small voice is the healer and the master of all wisdom inside of you. We have spent so much time silencing this voice to now turn to it to listen seems strained and odd. Like training for a great marathon the time of practice leads to great strength and endurance so continue to press forward and do not give up.

You will find yourself requiring this time of quite in order to have an enriched life of purpose and peace that you will be unable to be without. This will be your solace.

In Loving memory of the Rav P. Berg creator of the Kabbalah Centre International. (1927-2013)

Profound statements from his noted book on Kabbalah for the Laymen.

I give you this to help awaken your deep inner thoughts to develop your inner guidance and to hear from your heart on what it is you should or do not want to believe. These passages awakened something very deep in me and changed the way I view this world and the next. It also started a dream so big in my heart that I cannot pretend anymore that nothing is out there beyond this physical existence we call earth.

Please just read and meditate on the following and May you find your "aha moment".

Free Will: Thoughts and intentions create metaphysical molds into which we can pour the cement of physical manifestation.

Kabbalah is a goal-means system-the goal means, like space-time and energy-matter, are inseparable. By knowing the process, by living the process, one can understand the process from beginning to end. The more fully something is established in the mind, the better the chance for a successful completion. The entire process manifests first in the mind.

As we discussed earlier you must have the creative thought first then expand on it to bring it into this world. All creativity begins as a thought, good or bad.

Beyond common senses; The purpose of Kabbalah is to remove the chains of logic and reason so that we may be released from the cage of our five common senses, for it is only by transcending the limits of theses self-made linear boundaries that a direct link with the cosmic forces can be made. Only then can the real inner journey begin.

The mind is the defining barrier of all that is allowed to exist in what we call our world. Think on that, much of what we do is based on thought patterns that are self-taught or a creation of our environment. That is why you must exercise your free will to overcome the things that do not serve you.

Pressure; No longer can we close our eyes to the light of creation. The light is pressing in, instilling us with a sense of urgency, exhorting us on to greater and greater heights of consciousness, impelling us toward planetary consciousness. Now, more than ever, the Light of Creation demands revealment. There is only one way to relieve the pressure; Reveal the Light.

On this you come to understand that the pressure or nagging feeling we have inside that something is missing is the Light trying to manifests itself within you. But, you must permit this to become your new reality. Nothing is forced.

Altered States; Humanity thankfully, cannot cause chaos in the upper realms. Thus, our thoughts, if tempered by positive resistance, are virtually impervious to the petty machinations of those who are possessed by Desire to Receive for Oneself Alone. The illusion of negative space is here for a very real purpose, and that is to allow us the opportunity of bridging the gap between ourselves and the ultimate reality of the Light. Through conscious resistance and restriction one can transform the Desire to Receive for the Oneself Alone into Desire for the Sake of Sharing.

You can see in these statements how free will and using the technique of restriction can bring you the change you are desiring and the activation of the upper realms to bring that reality into existence with the power of your free will.

Faces of Evil; Evil has a thousand faces, and yet it has only one. From the perspective of the lower Seven Sefirot, evil is the like one of those miracle-do-all-plastic devices as advertised on late night TV. It can be sculpted, bent, and twisted, adjusted, amended, edited and revised, converted, corrected, modified, reversed and flip-flopped. Mold it, shape it, and wear it like a mask. Toss it like a salad. Shoot it from a gun. Con with it, cheat with it, hoodwink, rob and swindle. Tease it like a beehive hairdo. It lusts! It envies! Evil-what a versatile product! And, of course, it comes with a limited sixty second money back guarantee.

Those are but a few of the false faces of evil. In reality evil has but one face, the thought energy-intelligence of Desire to Receive for Oneself Alone. Everything that revolves around that deceptive, ever-changing face of Desire, everything that emanates from it, everyone who allows that negative aspect of Desire to prevail, falls under its influence.

Yet, evil has no life of its own. Like a puppet, it is a lifeless, bloodless entity onto which we paint the faces, and for which we pull the strings. We animate evil and give it substance through our negative thoughts and actions. As a result, we also have the prerogative of painting evil with an attractive face. Yes, despite its myriad dubious characteristics, even evil may be seen in a positive light. In fact, it may be said that evil is an Earthly necessity, for it is only through restriction of Desire to Receive for Oneself Alone that the Light is revealed. Perhaps, then, we owe a small debt of gratitude to evil for allowing us the opportunity of absolving Bread of Shame. Then again, perhaps we don't.

Yes, this puts us on the firing line, can it be me? All comes from within, good or bad as I stated before. Remember what I said earlier using the words of Jesus "The spirit is willing but the flesh is weak" To me that sums up all that needs to be said. So we now know that this is no surprise this **human nature**. This is our life's journey to bring the human spirit in to submission with the supernatural spirit in us. Bringing the life of Christ into the earthly realm with the gifts of the spirit, is truly heaven on earth.

Heaven down to earth. Living a heavenly life on earth, we are given free will. This is the power of choice.

The Middle Point; If we feel sadness or depravation it means that we are ensconced in illusion. As mentioned previously, lack can take root only in the world of illusion, and only there can it survive. By attaching to the Infinite Middle Point of our beings we cause the illusion of lack to lose its purpose in the world of illusion and, thus, having nothing of a negative nature on which to feed, it must of necessity disappear.

The importance of connecting with the Middle Point, humanity's internal place of Light's revealment, cannot be overemphasized. In fact, the Middle Point is generally accepted by the kabbalists as being the fundamental difference between the spiritual and the non-spiritual person. For whereas the spiritual person understands that all blessings emanate from a single source, the non-spiritual person sees only random chance as the motivating influence of his or her life. Thus, while the spiritual person's life is anchored in the tranquil waters of Reality, the non-spiritual person is tossed about like a twig on a sea of illusion.

Down and Out

It has been said to me that Depression is the manifestation due to a lack of faith. I now know that to be true. When I have had my deep moments of depression I was not practicing my faith and or reading or engaging in study; that lead to my vulnerability.

Your Ego wants to have the last say about everything. Practicing faith and doing positive thinking and doing actions that are good and helping others takes a very concentrated effort. If you have not done these things in the past it will take every ounce of your being to accomplish one skill at a time to create that new life style that you desire.

When you help yourself, you are now ready to help someone else. This will make you a better person in every area of your life. Your health will improve, your potential to learn will grow tremendously and you are now able to love freely knowing how loved you are from the Creator God.

You were meant to be someone great, do not let any situation steal another minute of the great life God has in store for you.

We all have moments of sadness that seem to linger or

appear out of nowhere. Again, the ego is fighting to retain negative ground. You having a great faith and acting and speaking in Love, is not the intention of the ego. It lust's for self-gratification, no matter the cost.

Starting the Never Ending Journey

So life as we know it is a "Constant" journey. Once we come to realize that every choice every decision has an unending ripple on everything around us and across the globe.

Having and embracing that can make all the difference in how your life is played out and who will be in that "play as well".

We are constantly creating our life, with no comprehension of the magnitude our will and choices made. Once you understand that you are the "Creator of your Life" you will never be asleep again at the wheel of your life.

Participation is the hardest training you will ever receive; it causes great joy and can also make us feel great pain. But, I do know from experience that knowledge is power and freedom.

The question is will you be bold enough to take that chance, or are you willing to miss the greatest opportunity this life has to offer you.

Try to recall why you choose this path to begin with, nothing is an accident. All of our struggles and pains bring our soul up the spiritual ladder of accession. Whether we realize it or not, your soul has only one goal and that is too ascend.

Why Love

This is the most profound mystery of all. This is the golden carrot that all of us want and desire on every level of our being.

Daily we reach out for approval and gratitude to just basic kindness, so we can fill that need. It comes in many different forms and sometimes we take it any way we can just to have a piece of it in our life. Sometimes we even take punishment over the long haul for the short burst of love that is bestowed on us.

This is where self-love has to be so strong that punishment of any sort is removed from our life because we realize that our need for Love can only be met by the One and only Creator God. He is our teacher, healer and most of all our mentor on how to be, act and feel loved. Upon creation that came out of Love due to our image and likeness of God, does it not make sense to you, why our desire is of the same essence as the Creator?

Why am I telling you all This

Because someone told me these things along with the help of the Angels and my life has never been the same since. I believed for so long that I was so alone here. Again a tool of the enemy to keep you down.

Sometimes the simple things need to be heard on a very simple format to click so we have our "Aha" moment.

Have you had yours yet? Does any part of what was mentioned resonate in your soul? Do you feel the calling deep inside your soul begging to be released?

Are you angry, un-fulfilled and have a nagging feeling that there has to be so much more to this life. This is your soul crying out to be rescued. The best part is that it only gets better from here. Your built in life preserver has been activated and is requesting your presence. Can you answer that call? Are you finally ready to let your soul be in charge and tell your ego once and for all who the real boss is!

This can be very liberating and more than a life change, it is magical what your decision can do no matter what your current situation is or what it looks like.

Start writing a new version of your movie and re write all the bad scripts and replace them with your new Love force of intention for a Life that is worth living and filled with nothing but, a deep passion to serve human kind and live a blessed life that has been given to us on this magnificent planet. Sound too far-fetched. It is not really you only have to change the movie running in your head. We are surrounded by so much beauty that we daily take for granted. Once you start looking you will never look back.

The Benefit of Gratitude

We live in a very fast past society that is constantly moving and expanding. Sometimes I feel if I keep my eyes closed to long that I will miss something. So the question is how do we keep up and slow down at the same time, without losing our most important asset ourselves?

Some of us are so busy doing for others. We are the ones left behind and feeling neglected. Through trial and error you can love yourself first and then reap the benefits and rewards that soon follow. This behavior is not selfish it must happen in order to live a life that is full-filling and one that can only exude thank-fullness and gratitude.

Your love will be expressed by learning to love yourself first. This love can only happen through much practice and a concentrated effort to make it happen that turns into habit.

Take the baby steps necessary to find the path of love that only you can express. Everyone's Love walk is different and original and cannot be copied by anyone.

Committing To Change

Now that you have made a decision to start making changes in your life with it comes the awesome task of where to start. This is where baby steps are very important because nothing will be rectified overnight. This thought should sit with you in a very calming way, for to eliminate the behavior slowly so that it is forever gone. I wish I could hand you the magic wand to make it all disappear but, then you would miss all the glorious healing that comes from the removal of the thing that has been dragging you down.

There is great peace to be had on the other side for all your hard work. Also the growth that comes with this process is so precious and priceless there are really no words to convey this to you. But, the feeling you have when you have achieved this will certainly be for you as beautiful and fulfilling as it was for me, and with that all that is left is Love.

I wish you much success on your journey and you are never alone. Many have felt the way you are feeling and many have overcome realizing that Love is the best medicine there ever was and it has always been inside of you, you just have to activate it and begin using it.

Love works in all areas of our lives and once you get a taste for it believe me you will crave it, and that's ok because it is so good for you, and you do not need to see a Doctor to get permission or and RX. As the saying goes "But most of all I wish you Love"

Ps Now re-write that list of 5 about yourself. Likes vs Dis-likes. Hopefully if you are reading this you are already thinking different than you were from the first list?

Baby Steps.......................

References

A) Amplified Bible by Zondervan Publishing house
Copyright 1987

B) Kabbalah for the Laymean by Rav Berg
First Edition 2012 Kabbalah Centre International, Inc.

C) The Complete Works by Florence Scovel Shinn (a must read)

The Dover Edition, First published in 2010. From original publication of the Game of Life and How to play it (1925), Your word is your word (1928) The secret door to success (1940) and the power of the spoken word (1945).

Library of congress cataloging-in-publication data Shinn, Florence Scovel, d. 1940 (Works 2010)

D) A must Read: The Angel Bible by Hazel Raven
Published by Sterling in 2006
Magnet-

(1) Footnote: Etymology.com. Under Magnesium and Ferromagnetic
(2) Footnote: The New American Webster's Dictionary.
Handy college-Third Edition by signet 1995

CPSIA information can be obtained
at www.ICGtesting.com
Printed in the USA
BVHW031428071119
563198BV00004B/23/P